Verena Mai

The capacity of welfare regimes to absorb macro-economic shocks

National differences in the development of unemployment, poverty and the distribution of income in the aftermath of the financial crisis 2008

Anchor Academic
Publishing

Mai, Verena: The capacity of welfare regimes to absorb macro-economic shocks. National differences in the development of unemployment, poverty and the distribution of income in the aftermath of the financial crisis 2008. Hamburg, Anchor Academic Publishing 2013

Buch-ISBN: 978-3-95489-150-4
PDF-eBook-ISBN: 978-3-95489-650-9
Druck/Herstellung: Anchor Academic Publishing, Hamburg, 2013

Bibliografische Information der Deutschen Nationalbibliothek:
Die Deutsche Nationalbibliothek verzeichnet diese Publikation in der Deutschen Nationalbibliografie; detaillierte bibliografische Daten sind im Internet über http://dnb.d-nb.de abrufbar.

Table of contents

List of Tables and Figures

Tables

Figures

'International economic crises are to countries what reagents are to compounds in chemistry: they provoke changes that reveal the connections between particularities and the general. If the comparativist can find countries subject to the same stresses, it then becomes possible to see how countries differ or converge and thereby to learn something about cause and effect'

- Peter Gourevitch: Politics in Hard Times (1986: 221)

1. Introduction

The financial crisis, which struck the EU countries in 2008, was followed by the severest economic recession since the end of the Second World War, involving a significant drop in GDP (negative economic growth) for most of them.[1] Output growth has turned negative or stagnated in several countries, the impact on labour markets has led to rising unemployment rates and public debt and deficits have soared.[2] In the aftermath of the crisis countries were confronted with a deteriorating social context, which is due to the severity of the economic downturn, the worsening job situation and the increased unemployment. This has resulted in a heightened need for social protection while at the same time making it more difficult to finance.[3]

The crisis has highlighted the role of social protection as a social buffer and an economic stabilizer that cushions the impact of recessions. Social benefits have been an essential element of national crisis response in the countries of the European Union.[4] Social security programmes not only act as an important component of the crisis „exit strategy“, helping to revitalize the economy but they also protect the most vulnerable part of society.[5] The sharp fall in employment and therefore disposable income affected some sectors of economy as well as some social groups much more than others.[6] One of the lessons that can be learned from the crisis is that countries and their inhabitants are differently exposed to economic shocks due to the variations in the design of social security that they are covered with.[7] This consideration is essential to analysis because, as Őzdemir et al (2010) point out, the origins of the crisis can be spotted in the financial sector, where income levels tend to be relatively high. Nevertheless, there is piecemeal evidence that the most vulnerable in society have to struggle most with the negative consequences of the crisis.[8]

[1] Cf. Euzéby (2010): 72
[2] Letschke et al. (2012): 243
[3] Cf. Euzéby (2010): 72
[4] Cf. Euzéby (2010): 71
[5] Cf. Konkolewsky (2009): 3
[6] Cf. Özdemir et al. (2010): 3
[7] Cf. Behrendt et al. (2011): 169
[8] Cf. Őzdemir et al. (2010): 3

This book examines the capacity of specific types of welfare states, classified mainly according to Esping-Andersen's concept, to absorb macro-economic shocks – in particular with reference to the most vulnerable parts of society. Which social policy challenges arise in Sweden, Austria and Spain and which differences in the economic and socio-political impacts of the crisis can be identified?

The question regarding the ability of a system to handle external disturbances gains importance, as one of the main claims after the outbreak of the financial crisis is to improve our political, economical and societal systems to become more resistant or resilient.[9] Resilience is defined as the ability of a system to withstand a major disruption within acceptable degradation parameters and to recover within an acceptable time, and composite costs, and risks.[10] The term originated in the field of ecology and describes how an ecological system can handle external disturbances and absorb changes in variables and parameters and still persist, like a forest regenerating after a fire.[11] A noteworthy remark to bear in mind for the following analysis is that both the concept of the business cycle and the term 'resilience' convey a degree of cyclical development. While the business cycle describes the periodical ups and downs of the economy[12], resilience is embedded in the theory of an adaptive cycle. This theory stresses development of dynamical systems such as ecosystems, societies and economies underlies a continuous and cumulative process, undergoing the four phases: rapid growth and exploitation, conservation, collapse or release and reorganisation.[13]

Identifying the social impact of the economic downturn for European countries in the aftermath of the financial crisis is not straightforward.[14] There are various direct and indirect consequences for individuals of a country. Therefore, the purpose of this analysis is to investigate three indicators of the downturn and their development in the middle term to highlight the impacts of the crisis from different perspectives. The first indicator analysed is the unemployment rate, which indicates the economic aspects of the crisis. The focus will be on analysing the consequences for employees with different levels of education and for the younger workforce (15-24 years) to identify whether these social groups have been especially affected by the crisis. Secondly, to investigate whether the economic downturn has heightened the danger to be affected by poverty, changes in the poverty rate will be presented for Sweden, Austria and Spain – each country representing a different type of welfare state. Finally, the analysis of the Gini coefficient shall show whether there have been shifts in the distribution of income within the society.

---

[9] Cf. http://www.zeit.de/2012/03/A-Analyse, Die Zeit (28.10.2012)
[10] Cf. Aven (2011): 517
[11] Cf. Holling *(1973):* 17f
[12] Cf. Burns; Mitchell (1946): 3f
[13] Cf. Carpenter (2001): 766
[14] Cf. Figari et al. (2010): 4

The approach adopted relates to the data from the European Labour Force Survey and those compiled by the EU-SILC to illustrate the consequences of the crisis – in particular with reference to the most vulnerable parts of society and the capacity of specific types of welfare states to absorb macro-economic shocks. Although, the investigation of the unemployment rate in combination with the poverty rate and the Gini coefficient reflects only a sub-area of the consequences that countries have to face it shall provide insights into national differences of the ongoing crisis. The goal is to test the hypothesis whether a specific type of welfare state model is more resilient to the impacts of the crisis than others.

2. Challenges for Three European Welfare States: Sweden, Austria and Spain

2.1. Welfare State Typology

Von Kempski (1972) defines the general term 'welfare state' as a class of democratic industrial capitalist societies, characterized by certain properties. These include for example social citizenship or the fact that more or less extensive welfare provisions are legally provided, or, in other words, the fact that the state plays a principal part in the welfare mix alongside the market, civil society, and the family.[15] According to Esping-Andersen (1990), this class of societies does not consist of a great number of unique cases but they cluster together in regime-types, which he defines according to their quality of social rights, social stratification, and the relationship between state, market, and family.[16] In his book 'The three worlds of welfare capitalism' he distinguishes between the liberal welfare state, the corporatist welfare state and the social-democratic welfare state.[17] Before continuing to outline the characteristics of each group in greater detail, it is essential to explain the connection of the welfare state typology and the further analysis.

Firstly, attention has to be paid to the fact that Esping-Andersen clusters the welfare states into these categories but points out that in the real world there are no one-dimensional nations. Core liberal elements for example can be found in predominantly social democratic states and vice versa, meaning that there are no one-dimensional nations.[18] With that in mind, the reader should be aware that this analysis does not intend to compare the welfare states and the intensity with which they have been hit by the crisis on scales of more or less as this would oversimplify a very complex issue. Instead, the country specific context has to be considered when we are trying to ask if one of the countries was more resilient against the negative impacts of the crisis than others.

Secondly, it is true that Esping-Andersen did not only receive acclaim for his work but also criticism. Critics argue that his typology is neither exhaustive nor exclusive and therefore needs revising.[19] Others even go one step further and point out that typologies as such have no explanatory power meaning that his scheme is not appropriate for theorizing about what is happening with and within welfare states.[20] Nevertheless, regarding the purpose of this article, Esping-Andersen's typology offers the distinctive advantage of giving a bird's eye view of the broad characteristics of a social or historical situation. Through the simplification

[15] Cf. Von Kemskpi (1972) as cited in Arts and Gelissen (2002): 139
[16] Cf. Esping-Andersen (1990): 29
[17] Cf. Esping-Andersen (1990): 26ff
[18] Cf. Esping-Andersen (1990): 28f
[19] Cf. Arts, Gelissen (2002): 139
[20] Cf. Baldwin (1996): 41

and aloofness from details it emphasizes on the essential features of a situation considered as a whole.[21] On these grounds, his categories will be the point of departure for this investigation although no country representing the liberal welfare state will be included due to the limited extent of this paper.

Finally, one important criticism of Esping-Andersen's classification is that he did not develop a separate cluster for the Mediterranean countries such as Spain, Portugal and Greece. Nevertheless, it has to be recognized that these countries have some important characteristics in common like the catholic imprint (with the exception of Greece) and a strong familialism.[22] Some commentators of his typology (Leibfried, 1992; Ferrera, 1996; Bonoli, 1997; Trifiletti, 1999) have developed classifications of European welfare states integrating a separate cluster for the 'southern model'.[23] I consider these states especially interesting when investigating the negative impacts of the crisis as they are - at the time of writing this paper - exceedingly present in the media and I will therefore include one representative of the Mediterranean countries, namely Spain, into the following analysis.

This book compares the social policy challenges arising in Spain (representing the Southern European welfare state), in Sweden (representing the social democratic-regime type) and in Austria (representing the conservative welfare state) and the capacity of each country to absorb macro-economic shocks.

---

[21] Cf. Ars, Gelissen (2002): 139
[22] Cf. Esping-Andersen, (1997): 180
[23] Cf. Arts, Gelissen (2002): 145

Sweden

Social democratic welfare state

The social democratic regime-type is named after the social democracy that was the predominant force behind social reforms. Beside Sweden, countries such as Denmark, Finland, the Netherlands and Norway belong to the category of social democratic welfare states. The principles of universalism and decommodification of social rights were extended to promote an equality of the highest standards. All social strata are incorporated under one universal insurance system and benefits are graded according to the level of earnings. This model represents a counterbalance to the market and, in contrast to the conservative welfare state, it does not follow the principle of subsidiarity. Thus, it does not wait until the family's capacity to aid is exhausted but to pre-emptively socialize the costs of familyhood.[24] Women in particular are encouraged to participate in the labour market. This system of generous universal and highly redistributive benefits is aimed at a maximization of capacities for individual independence. To ensure such a high-level solidaristic welfare system these types of welfare state regimes are dedicated to full employment.[25]

Austria

Conservative or corporatist welfare state

According to Esping-Andersen, Austria belongs, alongside other countries such as France, Germany and Italy, to the category of conservative welfare states. In these conservative and strongly 'corporatist' welfare states, the liberal obsession with market efficiency and commodification was never preeminent and, as such, the granting of social rights was hardly ever a seriously contested issue.[26] But the direct influence of the state is restricted to the provision of income maintenance benefits related to occupational status. As a result, the sphere of solidarity remains quite narrow.[27] According to Esping-Andersen, the market in these countries could be displaced as a provider of welfare by the state, which is illustrated by the marginal roles that private insurance and fringe benefits play. The conservative welfare state is historically shaped by the church and supports the preservation of traditional family. The principle of "subsidiarity" assures that the state will only interfere when the family's capacity to service its members is exhausted.[28]

[24] Cf. Esping-Andersen (1990): 27f
[25] Cf. Arts, Gelissen (2002): 142
[26] Esping-Andersen (1990): 27
[27] Cf. Arts, Gelissen (2002): 142
[28] Cf. Esping-Anders (1990): 27

Spain

Familialist or Southern European welfare state

Karamessini summarises findings from the lively discussion about the distinctiveness of a Southern European Model of social protection and welfare regime that goes back to the early 1990s.[29] She points out that family is still the cornerstone of this model – even labelling it 'the main social shock absorber'[30] – and the primary locus of solidarity when it comes to the provision of care and support[31]. Trifiletti argues that only certain risks are covered largely by the welfare state those against the family cannot protect itself.[32] Labour force groups such as women, young people and migrants suffer from high unemployment and are disproportionately involved in irregular forms of work. Social security is based on occupational status and work performance, and social assistance schemes are residual since those without a normal working career must primarily rely on the family for support. Furthermore, the family members and mainly women's unpaid work basically provide the care of children and elderly. Karamessini criticises that labour segmentation creates gaps and inequalities in both employment and social protection and that unemployment compensation is underdeveloped. Overall, welfare state institutions seem highly inefficient.[33] According to Ferrera, social protection systems of Southern countries are highly fragmented and, although there is no articulated net of minimum social protection, some benefits are very generous (such as old age pensions).[34]

Apart from merely understanding the basic characteristics of each welfare regime it is furthermore essential to consider changes that each country has undergone in the last two decades as well as outlining tensions before and to some extent after the outbreak of the crisis, which are summarised in the table below.

---

[29] Cf. Karamessini (2007): 2
[30] Cf. Karamessini (2007): 2
[31] Cf. Karamessin (2007): 5
[32] Cf. Trifiletti (1999): 49
[33] Cf. Karamessini (2007): 5
[34] Cf. Ferrera (1996): 4ff

Table 1 Overview of the specific welfare regimes, their characteristics and tensions before and after the outbreak of the financial crisis 2008

	Type of model	Relevant changes in the 1990s and 2000s	Tensions/unresolved issues before crisis	New trends/emerging tensions since 2008
Sweden	Social democratic welfare state	Revitalisation through reestablishment of model (macroeconomic controls, social contracts) plus new pillars, such as innovation	Combining labour standards with product market deregulation but under threat from EU. High taxes still a political challenge.	Core components of model only marginally modified, and rise in public deficit limited; but increasingly duality of labour market, deteriorating employment prospects for young people/immigrants/low skilled, weakening of trade unions through unemployment insurance reform
Austria	Conservative welfare state	Conversion – from demand-led to supply-led corporatism	Continuity of corporatism, with continuing regulation of labour standards associated with major changes in political context. Failure to modernise family and welfare policy.	Revival of social partnership, heightened dependency on exports and on Germany, banks highly dependent on CEE
Spain	Familialist welfare state	From CME (coordinated market economy) to liberal. Tensions between development and familialist model.	Liberalisation of model; strong dualisation of labour market. Some recent but limited changes to familialist welfare model. Reliance on housing market resulting in exposure to credit crunch.	After bursting of real estate bubble: very high (youth) unemployment, absence of industrial policy incl. vocational training, fragmentation of collective bargaining fostering low-wage strategies, significant public spending cuts, 'prospects are dramatic'

Source: adjusted illustration on basis of Lehndorff et al (2012): 12ff (Introduction)

2.2. A typology of economic crises

In discussing the effectiveness of welfare states concerning their resilience against the negative impacts of crises, it is necessary to know how a crisis in general can be distinguished from normal fluctuations or recessions in the business cycle, what the core-elements of such a crisis are and what different types of crises exist.

The most prominent example of an empirical characterisation of the business cycle is from Burns and Mitchell who summarise it as follows:

> "Business cycles are a type of fluctuation found in the aggregate economic activity of nations that organize their work mainly in business enterprises: a cycle consist of expansions occurring at about the same time in many economic activities, followed by similarly general recessions, contractions and revivals which merge into the expansion phase of the next cycle."[35]

A *recession,* as defined by the National Bureau of Economic Research (NBER), means a 'significant decline in economic activity spread across the economy, lasting more than a few months, normally visible in real GDP, real income, employment, industrial production, and wholesale-retail sales.[36] In contrast to a recession, the aggregate income decreases in absolute

[35] Burns; Mitchell (1946): 3

[36] http://www.nber.org/cycles.html, NBER (28.10.2012)

terms during depressions.[37] The main features of a depression include withholding of investment, rising unemployment, and falling prices and profits. [38]
An *economic crisis* in general is characterised by a sudden, and often unexpected, deterioration of most key macroeconomic indicators, including GDP growth, unemployment levels, inflation rates and public debt.[39] An economic crisis may be triggered when rational expectations are displaced or replaced by mania or speculative excess in financial markets.[40] Reinhart and Rogoff explain that recessions associated with crises are more severe in terms of duration and amplitude than the usual business cycle benchmarks of the post-World War II period. [41] Crises that are even part of a global phenomenon may be worse in the amplitude and volatility of the downturn. [42] An *international economic crisis* is triggered by an external shock and affects a large number of countries world-wide.[43] The current crisis, which can be seen as the most severe financial crisis since the Great Depression - in terms of both economic costs and geographical reach - was triggered by adverse events in the global financial markets starting in mid-2007. Almost all developed countries and most major emerging markets experienced high levels of financial stress and reduced economic activity.[44] Other post World-War II crises were either country-specific or at worst regional whereas the recent crisis is global in scope and far deeper.[45] This is because output, trade, equity prices, and other indicators behave much the same way for the world aggregates as they do in individual countries. A sudden stop in financing typically impacts on a large part of the world's public and private sector. [46] The global scope of the crisis has made it far more difficult for individual countries to grow their way out through higher exports or to smooth the consumption effects through foreign borrowing. [47] Examples from previous crises demonstrate that graduation from recurrent banking and financial crises is much more elusive.[48]

Typically, a *financial crisis* is characterised by large-scale defaults of financial and non-financial enterprises, usually accompanied by falling incomes and prices in the economy as a whole. Through financial and other economic interdependences the implications of such crises spread internationally.[49] Claessens et al. suggest in their work that the post-2007 crisis

[37] http://wirtschaftslexikon.gabler.de/Definition/depression.html), Gabler Verlag (28.11.2012)
[38] Cf. Jones (2001): 320
[39] Cf. Starke et al. (2011): 2
[40] Cf. Jones (2001): 259
[41] Cf. Reinhart; Rogoff (2009): 269f
[42] Cf. Reinhart; Rogoff (2009): 269f
[43] Cf. Starke et al. (2011): 2
[44] Cf. Claessens et al. (2010): 269
[45] Cf. Reinhart; Rogoff (2009): 233
[46] Cf. Reinhart; Rogoff (2009): 269f
[47] Cf. Reinhart; Rogoff (2009): 239
[48] Cf. Reinhart; Rogoff (2009): 283
[49] Cf. Jones (2001): 537

stemmed from multiple factors, some common to previous financial crises, others new.[50] The sharp (and unsustainable) increase of asset prices, credit booms that led to excessive debt burdens, and the build-up of marginal loans and systemic risks are typical indicators for financial crises in general.[51] Furthermore, the post 2007-crisis has some features that were not familiar to past crises. Sophisticated financial intermediaries and instruments, increased interconnectedness among financial markets and a strong role of household indebtedness are critical factors for the severity and breadth of the crisis.[52]

Without doubt, the U.S. financial crisis of 2007 spilled over into other markets like Germany and Japan through direct linkages.[53] The ferocity, with which the recession spread globally, starting in the fourth quarter of 2008, is one important difference from previous crises. The sudden stop in global financing rapidly extended to businesses around the world infecting the real economy.[54] This *contagion* can be defined as an episode in which there are significant immediate effects in a number of countries following an event. If these consequences evolve over a matter of hours or days, Kaminsky, Reinhart and Végh label them “fast and furious”.[55] The potential of a global economic crisis is intensified by the increasing integration of financial markets and the fact that modern information and communications technology permit panic and mania to be transmitted almost instantaneously from one market to another.[56]

The aftermath of severe financial crises share three characteristics: [57]

- The asset market collapses are deep and prolonged.
- The aftermath of banking crises is associated with profound declines in output and employment.
- The value of government debt tends to explode. The main cause of debt explosion is not the widely cited costs of bailing out and recapitalizing the banking system. The biggest driver of debt increases is the inevitable collapse in tax revenues and increase in social expenditure that governments suffer in the wake of deep and prolonged output contractions.

Social policy responses are designed directly in response to an economic crisis, or indirectly, to address the social and economic consequences of such a crisis. [58]

---

[50] Cf. Claessens et al. (2010): 270
[51] Cf. Claessens et al. (2010): 272
[52] Cf. Claessens et al. (2010): 274
[53] Cf. Claessens et al. (2010): 242
[54] Cf. Claessens et al. (2010): 240
[55] Cf. Kaminsky et al. (2003): 55
[56] Cf. Jones: (2001): 257
[57] Cf. Reinhart; Rogoff (2009): 224
[58] Cf. Starke et al. (2011): 2

2.3. Impacts of the financial crisis on national budgets (2007 – 2010)

This chapter provides an overview of the economic and social impacts of the global financial crisis for the countries of the European Union placing a focus on Sweden, Austria and Spain. A comparison of the developments of the GDP growth rate, of the total government revenue and expenditure and of general government debt is provided. This aims to illustrate the severity of the economic downturn and furthermore, the variations that arose from country to country.

Table 2 Real GDP growth rate – volume as percentage point change on previous year, 2007 – 2011

Real GDP growth rate - volume (%change on previous year)					
	2007	2008	2009	2010	2011
EU 27	3,2	0,3	-4,3	2,0	1,5
EU 15	3,0	0,0	-4,4	2,0	1,4
Sweden	3,3	-0,6	-5,0	6,2	3,9
Austria	3,7	1,4	-3,8	2,1	2,7
Spain	3,5	0,9	-3,7	-0,1	0,7

Source: Eurostat (online data code: tec00115)

Swedish real GDP growth rates dropped first in 2008 and reached their lowest mark of minus 5 per cent in 2009. Strikingly, recovery followed swift with positive growth rates of 6,2 per cent in 2010 and 3,9 per cent in 2011. In comparison, Austria's GDP growth rate turned negative by -3.8 per cent in 2009, but reached values of 2,1 per cent in 2010 and 2,7 per cent by 2011. Spain's GDP growth rate has suffered less compared to Sweden, Austria and the EU average. In 2009 it has reached its low water mark at -3,7 per cent before improving to -0,1 per cent in 2010 and 0,7 per cent in 2011.

In summary, although Swedish real GDP growth rates were more drastically affected than Spain's, Sweden experienced a relatively fast and strong rebound. In Austria real GDP growth rates deteriorated slower than in the other two countries, but the values for Spain and Austria were nearly at the same low levels in 2009. Nevertheless, Austria's real GDP growth rates recovered in the following years more significantly.

Table 3 Development of the total government revenue as a percentage of GDP, 2007 – 2010

Development of total government revenue (% of GDP)					% point ch
	2007	2008	2009	2010	2007 - 2010
EU 27	44,7	44,7	44,2	44,1	-0,6
EU 15	45,1	45,2	44,7	44,6	-0,5
Sweden	54,5	53,9	54	52,4	-2,1
Austria	47,6	48,3	48,7	48,1	0,5
Spain	41,1	37	35,1	36,3	-4,8

Source: Eurostat (online data code: gov_a_main)

Sweden has the highest total government revenue in percentage of GDP compared to Austria, Spain and the EU average. Those revenues decreased by 2,1 percentage points between 2007 and 2010 from 54,5 to 52,4 per cent. On the other hand, Austria's revenue has even experienced a slight upward trend from 47,6 to 48,1 per cent within the same time period. Spanish government revenues plunged the highest from 41,1 per cent in 2007 to 36,3 per cent in 2010. This might be traced back to the early turning point for rising unemployment in May 2007 in combination with the rapid monthly deterioration. (Compare Figure 1 below and Appendix 1.)

Table 4 Development of the total government expenditure as a percentage of GDP, 2007 – 2010

Development of total government expenditure (% of GDP)					% point ch
	2007	2008	2009	2010	2007 - 2010
EU 27	45,6	47,1	51,1	50,6	5
EU 15	45,9	47,6	51,6	51,1	5,2
Sweden	51	51,7	54,9	52,5	1,5
Austria	48,6	49,3	52,9	52,6	4
Spain	39,2	41,5	46,3	45,6	6,4

Source: Eurostat (online data code: gov_a_main)

Although the three countries investigated as well as the EU average increased their total government expenditure (in percentage of GDP) after the outbreak of the financial crisis and reached their highest spending level in 2009, the intensity of this increase varied greatly from country to country. In 2007, Sweden's level of total government expenditure in percentage of GDP is well above the EU average with 51 per cent (EU15: 45,9%; EU27: 45,6%) and the levels of Austria (48,6%) and Spain (39,2%). Sweden, however, has only slightly raised its expenditures with a maximum of 54,9 per cent in 2009 before cutting back to 52,5 per cent and an overall increase between 2007 and 2010 of merely 1,5 percentage points.

Austria ramped up its government expenditure almost steadily from 48,6 per cent to 52,6 per cent between 2007 and 2010. Whereas this heightening is still below the increase of 5 percentage points in the EU27, Austria's total level of government expenditure has been the highest among our observed countries in 2010, even outrunning Sweden.

Out of the investigated countries Spain clearly has the lowest rates of government expenditure in percentage of GDP. Yet, in the aftermath of the financial crisis, those expenditures have increased drastically from only 39,2 per cent in 2007 to 45,6 per cent in 2010. This increase of 6,4 percentage points is the largest among the three observed countries and larger than the EU average.

After discussing whether and to what extent governments have increased their expenditures in the immediate aftermath of the crisis, the next concern consequently is the purpose of this government spending. A helpful starting point for this consideration is the data collection of Eurostat on general government expenditure by economic function according to the international Classification of the Functions of Government (COFOG).[59] The four clusters having the highest relevance for this investigation are displayed for each individual country in the table below.

Table 5 General government expenditure by its main function as a percentage of GDP, 2007 – 2010

General government expenditure by main function in percentage points of GDP						
		2007	2008	2009	2010	% point ch
General Public Service	EU 27	6,2*	6,3*	6,5*	6,5*	0,3
	EU 15	6,2*	6,4*	6,6*	6,6*	0,4
	Sweden	7,4	7,5	7,2	7,0	-0,4
	Austria	6,8	6,5	6,9	6,8	0,0
	Spain	4,6*	4,8	5,3	5,2	0,6
Economic Affairs	EU 27	3,9*	4,3*	4,6*	4,7*	0,8
	EU 15	3,7*	4,2*	4,5*	4,6*	0,9
	Sweden	4,0	4,2	4,7	4,6	0,6
	Austria	4,9	5,3	5,4	5,7	0,8
	Spain	5,1*	5,3	5,6	5,2	0,1
Health	EU 27	6,7*	7*	7,6*	7,5*	0,8
	EU 15	6,9*	7,1*	7,8*	7,6*	0,7
	Sweden	6,6	6,9	7,4	7,1	0,5
	Austria	7,5	7,8	8,3	8,1	0,6
	Spain	5,7*	6,1	6,8	6,5	0,8
Social Protection	EU 27	17,6*	18*	20*	19,9*	2,3
	EU 15	17,9*	18,4*	20,3*	20,3*	2,4
	Sweden	21,1	21,1	22,9	21,6	0,5

[59] Cf.http://epp.eurostat.ec.europa.eu/statistics_explained/index.php/General_government_expenditure_statistics; Eurostat a) (28.10.2012)

	Austria	19,8	19,8	21,8	21,7	1,9
	Spain	13,1*	14,1	16,3	16,9	3,8

** provisional*
Source: Eurostat (online data source: gov_a_exp)

Governmental spending on social protection, health and economic affairs has particularly risen since 2009. Clearly this reflects social and economic policy interventions in response to the crisis. In the EU as a whole, as well as in all individual member states, social protection is the most important function of government expenditure. It includes spending on sickness and disability, old age, family and children, unemployment, housing in the form of benefits in kind, and social exclusion.[60] However, distinct differences concerning the percentage spent by each government before and after the outbreak of the financial crisis are evident. Whereas Spain has only spent 13,1 per cent of its government expenditures on social protection in 2007, the levels of Austria and Sweden are with respectively 19,8 and 21,1 per cent of their GDP clearly above the EU average (EU27: 17,6%; EU15: 17,9%). Interestingly, those countries with a high level at the beginning of the crisis experienced only a slight increase of their social protection level between 2007 and 2010 (Austria: + 1,9 percentage points; Sweden: + 0,5 percentage points). Spain, on the contrary, has faced a drastic rise of 3,8 percentage points. Hence, it has used more than half of its increase of government expenditure (+6,4 percentage points between 2007 and 2010, compare Table 4) for social protection.

[60] Cf.http://epp.eurostat.ec.europa.eu/statistics_explained/index.php/General_government_expenditure_statistics; Eurostat a) (28.10.2012)

Table 6 General government debt as percentage of GDP and Public balance as percentage of GDP, 2007 - 2010

	General government debt (% of GDP)*				%point ch
	2007	2008	2009	2010	2007 - 2010
EU 27	59	62,5	74,8	80	21
Sweden	40,2	38,8	42,6	39,4	-0,8
Austria	60,2	63,8	69,5	71,9	11,7
Spain	36,3	40,2	53,9	61,2	24,9

	Public balance**				%point ch
	2007	2008	2009	2010	2007 - 2010
EU 27	-0,9	-2,4	-6,9	-6,5	-5,6
Sweden	3,6	2,2	-0,7	0,3	-3,3
Austria	-0,9	-0,9	-4,1	-4,5	-3,6
Spain	1,9	-4,5	-11,2	-9,7	-11,6

**general government consolidated gross debt*
***net borrowing/lending of consolidated general government sector*
Source: Eurostat (online data code: gov_dd_edpt1)

In Spain, the widening gap between total government revenues and total government expenditures consequently led to a severe deterioration of public balances. Within only four years (2007 – 2010) Spain's public balance suffered a decrease of 11,6 percentage points whereas Austria and Sweden experienced more moderate decreases of 3,6 respectively 3,3 percentage points within the same time period.

The basic level as well as the development of the general government consolidated gross debt, varies enormously from country to country. On average, government debt has increased by 21 percentage points between 2007 and 2010 in the EU27. While Spain had the lowest level of general public debt, its debt almost doubled within only four years from 36,3 per cent in 2007 to 61,2 per cent of GDP in 2010. Yet, Spain's overall level is with 61,2 per cent of general government debt in 2010 well below the EU27 average of 80 per cent and Austria's level of 71,9 per cent. Surprisingly, Sweden was – despite the difficult economic situation – able to improve its general debt by 0,8 percentage points between 2007 and 2010.

3. Impact of the Crisis on Unemployment, Poverty and Distribution

3.1. Unemployment: Developments in Sweden, Austria and Spain in comparison

Given the severity of the Great Recession, it is expected to have impacts on living standards on a scale not seen for almost 80 years. However, the role of governments and the extent of welfare states have developed enormously since the Great Depression in the 20th century, and partly this development has been in response to events following the Black Friday. Instruments of economic and social policy that have been developed would indicate that we are better equipped to deal with a deep downturn.[61]

A critical macroeconomic indicator of recessions is the level of unemployment. Indeed, this is likely to be one of the most important mechanisms through which recessions affect living standards.[62] However, the full impact of a recession may not feed through to living standards until several quarters after the recession officially begins as unemployment is a so-called `lagging indicator`.[63]

Selected data from the European Labour Force Survey 2007 until 2010 are used to illustrate the extent to which unemployment increased in the aftermath of the outbreak of the crisis and to spot variations in the effect concerning age groups and the level of education.

3.1.1. Unemployment rate of the total population (from 15 to 74 years)

The Labour Force Survey comprises all persons 15 to 74 years of age (16 to 74 in Spain) who were not employed during the reference week, had actively sought work during the past four weeks and were ready to begin working immediately or within two weeks.[64] As a result of the global economic crisis unemployment has risen sharply in the European Union. Every member state is affected by this surge. Nevertheless, the severity varies widely between countries and population subgroups. In the EU as a whole the unemployment began rising in March 2008, whereas the individual member states faced the onset of the rising unemployment at very different points in time. The fact that the member states structure and regulate their labour markets very differently from one another is one explanation for this phenomenon. In Spain, unemployment started to rise already in May 2007, whereas Austria and Sweden faced their turning point in the second quarter of 2008.[65] Not only the starting points

[61] Cf. Jenkins et al. (2011): 1-1
[62] Muriel; Sibieta (2009): 7
[63] Muriel; Sibieta (2009): 9
[64] http://epp.eurostat.ec.europa.eu/portal/page/portal/employment_unemployment_lfs/methodology/definitions; Eurostat c) (28.11.2012)
[65] Cf. Eurostat (2009): 1f

of the deterioration but also the further development of the unemployment rate show some interesting differences as illustrated in figure 1 below.

Figure 1 Illustration of the unemployment rate: monthly average, seasonally adjusted date, total population up to 74 years; 2007 – 2010

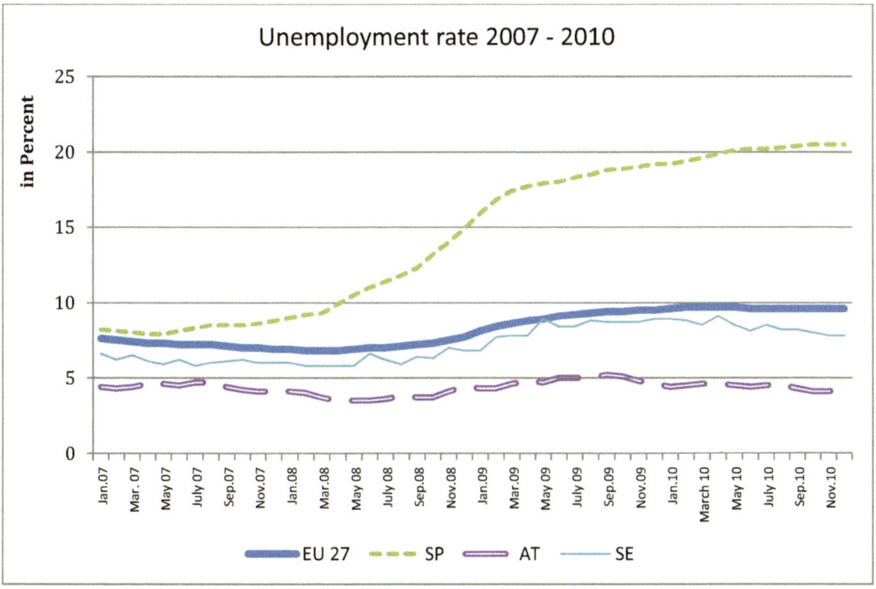

*Source: Eurostat (*une_rt_m)

Spain was the first country where the worsening economic situation led to increasing rates of unemployment. Since May 2007 the country experienced a continuously downward trend. The labour market in Spain has been hit hard by the economic crisis. An early turning point for a rise in unemployment (May 2007), in combination with rapid monthly expansion, is responsible for the increase from 8,2 per cent (January 2007) to 20,5 per cent (December 2010) of the unemployment rate[66] In December 2010, the last year of this investigation, unemployment stood at 20,5 per cent with no relief in sight. At the time of writing, the latest available data for Spain announce an unemployment rate of 25,1 per cent in August 2012.[67]
Sweden's unemployment rate started to rise in August 2008 from 5,9 per cent and experiences unsteady up- and downward movements peaking in April 2010 at 9,1 per cent. Since then, the unemployment rate slightly recovered and decreased until December to 7,8 per cent.
The unemployment rate in Austria was by far more constant. At all periods analysed it was well beneath the unemployment rates of Spain, Sweden and the EU average. It was not until October 2008 that the unemployment rate started responding to the deteriorating economic

[66] Cf. Eurostat (2009): 4
[67] Continous developments are displayed on the Eurostat datatable: une_rt_m

context. It rose slightly but steadily from 3,7 per cent in October 2008 until it peaked approximately one year later, in September 2009, at still very low 5,2 per cent. Since then it improved continuously reaching 4,2 per cent in December 2010.

3.1.2. Youth unemployment rate and youth unemployment ratio

A decisive pillar of this work focuses on youth unemployment as it has faced a substantial increase, especially in the industrialized countries.[68] Youth unemployment was on the rise in the EU27 since the first quarter of 2008, in line with total unemployment. Nevertheless, youth unemployment rates are significantly higher than total unemployment rate in the Member States and young people can be identified as a social group being especially vulnerable to those developments.[69]

Figure 2 Illustration of the unemployment rate: monthly average, seasonally adjusted date, population under the age of 25 years, 2007 – 2010

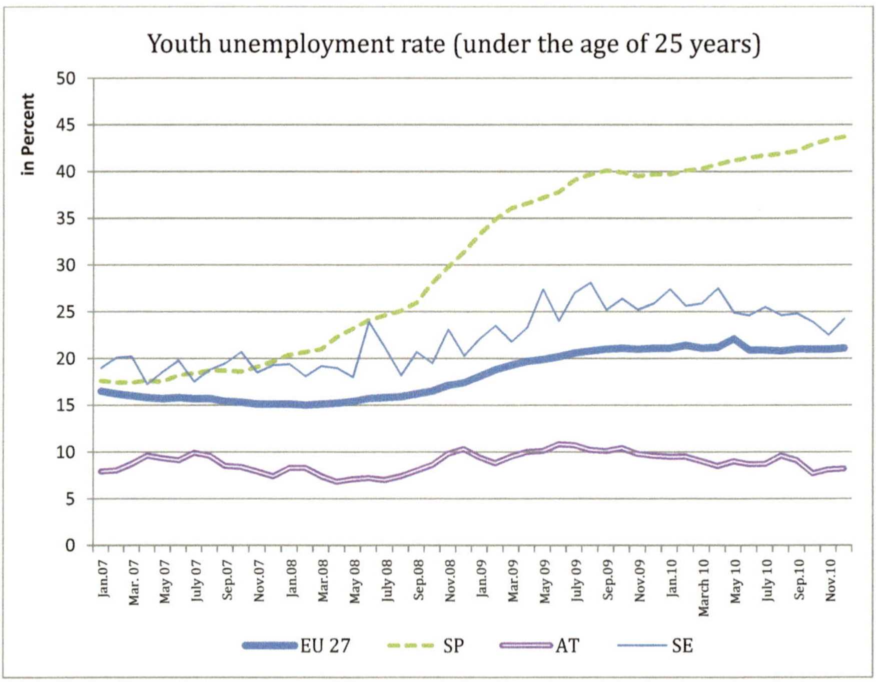

*Source: Eurostat (*une_rt_m)

[68] Cf. ILO (2012): 12
[69] Cf. Eurostat (2009): 6

In Spain the youth unemployment rate more than doubled between January 2007 (17,6%) and December 2010 (43,7%). In Sweden it rose from 19 per cent at the beginning of 2007 – peaking at 28,1 per cent in August 2009 - to 24,2 per cent in 2010 being still far away from pre-crisis levels. Indeed, in Austria the level of youth unemployment rate increased only slightly – despite the crisis – from 7,9 per cent (January 2007) to 8,2 per cent in December 2010. It reached its highest level of 10,8 per cent in June 2009 before it steadily declined.

There is, however, some discussion about the methodology with which the numbers for the youth unemployment are derived. Critics are questioning the validity of the youth unemployment rate and stating that it may misrepresent the true level of unemployment making it look far worse than it is. Taking these concerns serious, this book also takes a closer look at the youth unemployment ratio in addition to the youth unemployment rate, and the reasons why the first one may have more validity.

As mentioned above the adult jobless rate is calculated as the percentage of unemployed workers divided by the number of total workers in the labour force. For example 20 jobless workers and 200 workers in the labour force would mean an unemployment rate of 10 per cent. When calculating the youth unemployment rate, those attending university or job-training full-time are not considered part of the labour force because they are neither working nor looking for a job. As a result, millions of students are removed from the labour force making the denominator in the equation much smaller and, with the numerator staying the same, the unemployment rate looking higher. Assuming that in the example above, 150 out of the 200 workers enter university, they would no longer be counted as part of the labour force. Although the number of young people actually out of work has not changed, the unemployment rate has quadrupled to 40 per cent.

An alternative way of calculation is the youth unemployment ratio comparing the number of unemployed youth to the total population of young people under 24 years. Although Eurostat calculates the youth joblessness using both methodologies, the youth unemployment rate is widely reported.[70] But as we see when comparing both numbers further below there are vast differences, arising just from a change in methodology.

[70] Cf. http://www.ft.com/intl/cms/s/0/5cc9db3e-bbbc-11e1-9436-00144feabdc0.html#axzz2AVny80dq; Financial Times (28.10.2012)

Table 7 Illustration of the youth unemployment rate and youth unemployment ratio, population under the age of 25 years, 2007 – 2010

	Youth unemployment rate				Youth unemployment ratio			
	2007	2008	2009	2010	2007	2008	2009	2010
EU 27	15,7	15,9	20,1	21,1	6,8	6,9	8,7	9
EU 15	15,4	16	20,1	20,6	7,2	7,4	9,3	9,3
Spain	18,2	24,7	37,8	41,6	8,7	11,7	17,1	17,8
Austria	8,7	8	10	8,8	5,3	4,9	6	5,2
Sweden	19,1	20,1	25	25,2	10,1	10,7	12,8	13

Source: Eurostat (lfsi_act_a, une-rt_q)

The youth unemployment ratio has increased mostly in Spain from 8,7 per cent to 17,8 per cent followed by Sweden who has suffered an increase from 10,1 per cent to 13 per cent. Austria has experienced the most stable development with even a little decrease from 5,3 per cent in 2007 to 5,2 per cent in 2010.

It is worth mentioning that, while the EU15 youth unemployment rate has increased from 2009 to 2010, the youth unemployment ratio has stayed the same – although both measures are well above pre-2008 levels.[71] The differences between those two calculations are enormous indicating that the picture is not as bleak as it is always painted. Still, youth unemployment ratios of 17 per cent in Spain are nothing to feel complacent about. The dramatic situation is illustrated by the graphic below showing the increase of disillusioned young people (15 – 24 years) who do not think that there are jobs available. This group more than tripled from 2007 (0,5%) to 2010 (1,7%).

[71] Cf. http://www.ft.com/intl/cms/s/0/5cc9db3e-bbbc-11e1-9436-00144feabdc0.html#axzz2AVny80dq; Financial Times (28.10.2012)

Figure 3 Illustration of the percentage of inactive people between 15 – 24 years thinking no jobs are available in Spain, 2007 – 2010

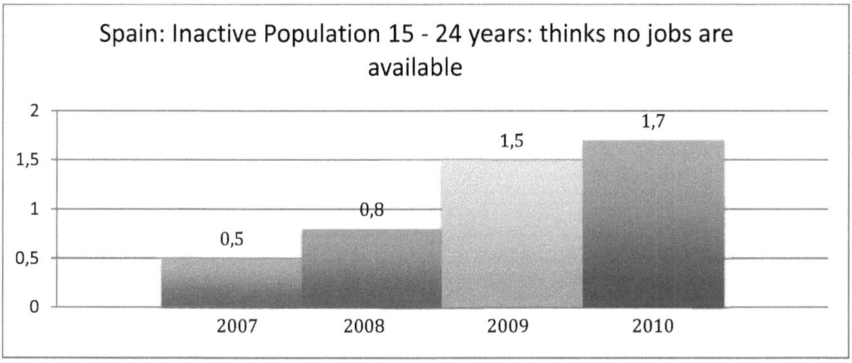

Source: Eurostat (lfsa_jpga)

3.1.3. Unemployment rate according to the highest level of education

Generally speaking it can be observed that education is the best insurance against unemployment. On the individual level, the unemployment risk arguably increases the lower the level of education attained.[72] Nevertheless, huge differences can be identified between the selected countries as displayed in the graphics below.

Table 8 Illustration of the unemployment rate by the highest level of education attained, population between 15 – 74 years, 2007 - 2010

Unemployment rate by the highest level of education attained				
	population btw. 15-74 years			
		level 0-2	level 3-4	level 5-6
EU 27	2007	10,6	6,9	4
	2008	11,3	6,5	3,8
	2009	14,5	8,3	5
	2010	15,8	9	5,4
EU 15	2007	10,3	6,6	4,1
	2008	11,2	6,5	4
	2009	14,5	8,2	5,1
	2010	15,8	8,5	5,4

[72] Cf. http://epp.eurostat.ec.europa.eu/statistics_explained/index.php/Unemployment_statistics#Further_Eurostat_information; Eurostat d) (accessed 28.10.2012)

Spain	2007	10,5	8,1	5,3
	2008	15,3	10,6	6,3
	2009	24,6	17,1	9,7
	2010	27,3	19,2	11,3
Austria	2007	8,6	3,7	2,5
	2008	7,8	3,3	1,7
	2009	9,8	4,1	2,3
	2010	8,5	3,9	2,4
Sweden	2007	11,6	5,1	3,6
	2008	12,2	5	3,4
	2009	16,2	7,6	4,4
	2010	17,6	7,6	4,5

Level 0-2: pre-primary, primary and low secondary education
Level 3-4: upper secondary and post secondary non-tertiary education
Level 5-6: first and second stage of tertiary education

Source: Eurostat (lfsa_urgaed)

Whereas citizens with a university degree, represented through level 5 and 6, were hardly affected by the crisis in Austria (-0,1 percentage points) and Sweden (+0,9 percentage points), the unemployment rate amongst academics in Spain more than doubled between 2007 and 2010 to reach 11,3 per cent in 2010. People with an upper secondary and post secondary non-tertiary education (level 3 and 4) felt the consequences on the labour market even stronger. The highest increase of 11,1 percentage points is observed in Spain, Sweden following clearly behind with an increase of 2,5 percentage points and in Austria the level is in 2010 0,2 percentage points above the pre-crisis level of 2007.

Without doubt, people with pre-primary, primary and low secondary education (level 0-2) are mostly affected by the drastical surge in unemployment. In all three countries as well as on the EU average, in 2007 unemployment was at least twice as high amongst graduates from compulsory school than among graduates from the tertiary education sector and in the aftermath of the crisis this gap widens continuously. In Spain, the unemployment rate in this educational level nearly tripled from 10,5 per cent in 2007 to 27,3 per cent in 2010. Sweden faced an increase of 6 percentage points, while in Austria even workers with a lower education seem to be well protected. After a surge from 7,8 per cent in 2008 to 9,8 per cent in 2009, the unemployment rate decreased again to 8,5 per cent in 2010.

Turning to the age group between 15 and 24, we see in Table 9 on page 24 that the pattern observed above repeats itself. In other words, in all countries – expect Austria – young people with higher education are better protected from the danger of becoming unemployed. Hence, the highest increase of unemployment can be observed among graduates from compulsory school. From 2007 until 2010, the unemployment rate for this group of young adults increases mostly in Spain by 29,2 percentage points, followed by Sweden with an increase of 9,4 percentage points and in the EU-15 it increases by 7,7 percentage points. In Austria unemployment in this group at first rises to 14,3 per cent in 2009 before it starts decreasing to 11,8 per cent in 2010 which is even below its 2007 pre-crisis level (12,4 per cent) and well below the levels of Spain (49,6 per cent) and Sweden (38,9 per cent). Nevertheless, it is noticeable that especially since 2009 unemployment is no longer confined to the lower educational level but that we can identify a rise amongst graduates from the tertiary sector. Especially in Spain, this group was highly affected and unemployment rose by 10,1 percentage points from 2008 to 2009. In the meantime, in the EU-27 young people with an academic degree experienced a rise in unemployment of 3,8 percentage points and in Sweden a rise of 1,1 percentage points. Unfortunately, Eurostat provides no comparable data for this group in Austria.

Table 9 Illustration of the unemployment rate by the highest level of education attained, population between 15 – 24 years, 2007 – 2010

Unemployment rate by the highest level of education attained				
	population between 15 - 24 years			
		level 0-2	level 3-4	level 5-6
EU 27	2007	20	13,4	11,4
	2008	21,2	12,9	11,7
	2009	26,1	17,1	15,5
	2010	27,5	18,1	16,3
EU 15	2007	19,7	12,1	10,7
	2008	20,9	12,4	11,1
	2009	25,9	16,2	14,9
	2010	27,4	16,6	15,3
Spain	2007	20,4	16,6	13,6
	2008	29,7	19,6	15,9
	2009	44,7	31,1	26
	2010	49,6	34,3	28,9

Austria	2007	12,4	6,2	*
	2008	12,1	5,7	*
	2009	14,3	7,5	*
	2010	11,8	7,1	*
Sweden	2007	29,5	12,1	12,3**
	2008	31,2	11,8	11,6**
	2009	38	18,4	12,7**
	2010	38,9	18,7	14,6

Level 0-2: pre-primary, primary and low secondary education
Level 3-4: upper secondary and post secondary non-tertiary education
Level 5-6: first and second stage of tertiary education
(no comparable data available for level 5 – 6 in Austria)
*Source: Eurostat (lfsa_urgaed); *not available / ** not reliable*

3.2. Poverty: Developments in Sweden, Austria and Spain in comparison

As unemployment rates were on the rise in all three countries it is important to understand to which extent the newly unemployed are protected from the risk of poverty by the specific social policy of their welfare regime. This book alludes to the argument that poverty rates are more comprehensive in measures of economic well-being than solely considering employment status or labour earnings.

It is expected that the degree to which poverty rises during an economic downturn will vary significantly across countries reflecting their different labour markets and socioeconomic institutions.[73] The aim of this section is to identify the factors and their respective impact, which prevent incomes from falling below the poverty threshold as this allows it to assess the effectiveness of social protection schemes.[74] Therefore it is inquired whether the economic recession has raised the relative number of poor people in Sweden, Austria and Spain in the midterm (2007 – 2010). To this end I first pose the question who is at risk of poverty meaning that their income is below 60% of the median equivalised income after social transfers. Apart from merely looking at the developments of poverty for the total population a closer look is taken at groups in society, which one would expect to be especially vulnerable to the impacts of the crisis to obtain a more differentiated picture. Detailed investigation will therefore be made for young people between 15 and 24 years, elderly people over 65 years and single parents with one dependent child.

Before comparing the relative poverty rates of different years I have to point out that the at-risk-of-poverty rate is a relative measure of poverty and the poverty threshold varies greatly

[73] Cf. Jenkins et al. (2011): 1-18
[74] Cf. Figari et al. (2010): 4, 8

between the different states.[75] Furthermore reductions in income due to unemployment result in some reduction to median incomes and consequently to the poverty threshold that is responsive to income changes. This decreased relative poverty threshold will - other things being equal - reduce the numbers of people counted as poor.[76] It is therefore necessary not only to look at the poverty rates but also at the development of the poverty threshold.

Table 10 At-risk-of-poverty threshold defined as 60% of median equivalised income for a single person, 2007 – 2010

At-risk-of-poverty threshold (60% of median equivalised income), single person				
	2007	2008	2009	2010
Spain	7,223	7,770	7,980	7,818
Austria	10,893	11,406	11,931	12,371
Sweden	11,307	12,344	12,749	11,825

Source: SILC, Eurostat (online data code: ilc_li01)

It can be observed that Austria is the only country whose poverty threshold has continuously risen from 10.893€ in 2007 to 12.371€ in 2010. Sweden and Spain, on the contrary, suffer from deteriorating income levels since 2009. In Spain, where the poverty threshold was already at a low level in 2007 (7.223€) in comparison to Austria (10.893€) and Sweden (11.307€) the poverty threshold fell between 2009 and 2010 by 162€. In Sweden where the poverty threshold was the highest among our investigated countries in 2007 it decreased by almost 1000€ between 2009 and 2010. However, It is not surprising that the falls in average income appeared with a time lag as unemployment is a lagging indicator of recessions[77] and earned income is the largest component in household's income packages on average.[78]

Table 11 At-risk-of-poverty rate defined as 60% of median equivalised income after social transfer for different groups of society, 2007 – 2010

At risk of poverty rate (60% of median equivalised income after social transfer)					
	Men & Women, total population				% point ch
	2007	2008	2009	2010	2007-2010
EU 27	16,5*	16,4	16,3	16,4	-0,1
EU 15	16*	16,2	16,1	16,2	0,2
Spain	19,7	19,6	19,5	20,7	1
Austria	12	12,4	12	12,1	0,1
Sweden	10,5	12,2	13,3	12,9	2,4

[75] Cf. Eurostat (2010): 1
[76] Cf. Figari et al. (2010): 11f
[77] Cf. Muriel; Sibieta (2009): 16
[78] Cf. Jenkins et al. (2011): 0-i

	Men & Women, 16 - 24 years				% point ch
	2007	2008	2009	2010	2007-2010
EU 27	20,8*	20,2	20,5	21,5	0,7
EU 15	20,6*	20,2	20,7	21,8	1,2
Spain	19,6	21,6	21	25,3	5,7
Austria	12,7	11,8	11,8	13,1	0,4
Sweden	24,7	24,9	26,3	26,9	2,2
	Men & Women, 65 years or over				% point ch
	2007	2008	2009	2010	2007-2010
EU 27	18,4*	19	18	16	-2,4
EU 15	18,9*	19,2	18	16,3	-2,6
Spain	28,2	27,4	25,2	21,7	-6,5
Austria	14	15	15,1	15,2	1,2
Sweden	9,9	15	17,7	15,5	5,6
	Single Person with dependent child				% point ch
	2007	2008	2009	2010	2007-2010
EU 27	33,1	35,4	33,8	36,6	3,5
EU 15	33	35,4	33,7	36,9	3,9
Spain	34,1	38,6	36,7	45,5	11,4
Austria	31,1	26,3	29,2	28,2	-2,9
Sweden	25	26,8	28,9	33,1	8,1

** Eurostat estimate*
Source: SILC, Eurostat (online data code: ilc_li02)

3.2.1. Poverty rate of the total population

When looking at poverty rates of the total population of our selection of countries, we discover that the pre-crisis level varies widely. Sweden has clearly the lowest rate of poverty (10,5 per cent) while at the same time having the highest poverty threshold (11.307€). In other words, those people counted poor in Sweden would partly not be counted poor in Spain as there the threshold lies distinctly lower at 7.223€. Despite Spain's relatively low poverty threshold, 19,7 per cent of the population are counted poor, which is clearly higher than the EU 15 (EU 27) figure of 16 (16,5) per cent. Austria also has relatively low poverty rates (12,4 per cent) while having a relatively high threshold of 10.893€.

When comparing the pathway of each country we uncover interesting differences. Spain experiences a nearly continuous upward trend of its poverty rate with an overall increase of one percentage point from 19,7 per cent in 2007 to 20,7 per cent in 2010. During the same time, Sweden's poverty rate increases from 10,5 per cent to it's highest level of 13,3 per cent in 2009 before decreasing slightly back to 12,9 per cent in 2010. Hence, Sweden has overall experienced the strongest increase of poverty with 2,4 percentage points.

Interestingly, in Austria the economic crisis does not seem to be reflected in the poverty rates at all. While Spain and Sweden experience an explicit increase, Austria's poverty rates rises only slightly from 12 per cent in 2007 to 12,4 per cent in 2008 before decreasing again. Overall, in 2010 the rate is only 0,1 percentage points higher than it has been before the crisis hit. When comparing Austria's development directly to Sweden, the effect gets even more obvious. Due to the strong resilience to the financial crisis 2008 and the following economic downturn, or, in other words, given the faster recovery, in 2010 Austria has overhauled Sweden both in terms of the height of the poverty threshold (AT: 12,371€; SE: 11,825€) and the percentage of people counted as poor (AT: 12,1%; SE: 12,9%). Meaning that in Austria – despite the financial and economic crisis - the median equivalised income has risen steadily while the poverty rate has nearly stagnated.

3.2.2. Youth-poverty rate

In the previous section one focus was the development of the youth unemployment rate. This indicator is highly critical as it is only the tip of the iceberg and illustrates the insecurity and vulnerability of young adults. Young people are disproportionately often affected by decent work deficits and low-quality jobs resulting in the phenomena of working poor, informal employment status and low pay.[79] Hence, I will analyse the poverty rates of men and women between 16 and 24 years to identify whether the heightened unemployment rates in this section are reflected by the poverty rates.

First, in 2007, it can be observed that the poverty rates of this age group are in all three countries studied, as well as in the EU-27 and EU-15 average, higher than the poverty rates of the total population. The lowest difference between the poverty rate of the total population and the age group of 16 to 24-year old can be spotted in Austria where it is with 12,7 per cent only slightly higher. What might come as a surprise is the especially high youth poverty rate in Sweden (24,7 per cent) which lies drastically above the EU-27 (EU-15) average of 20,8 per cent (20,6 per cent). Spain is slightly below these averages with a youth poverty rate of 19,6 per cent.

When analysing the development of the poverty rate of the 16 to 24-year old, it is noticeable that Sweden and Spain not only have a drastically higher level of young people being at-risk-of poverty to begin with but the poverty rate among young adults has also worsened more drastically than in Austria. While Sweden faces a steadily increase of 2,2 percentage points from 24,7 per cent in 2007 to 26,9 per cent in 2010 Spain's rate increases 5,7 percentage points from 19,6 per cent to 25,3 per cent in 2010. In the meantime, Austria's youth unem-

[79] Cf. ILO (2012): 13

ployment rate increases only slightly from 12,7 per cent in 2007 to 13,1 per cent in 2010 – approximately half the youth unemployment rate than the other two countries face.

3.2.3. Old-age poverty rate

Apart from the youngest in our society, the elderly are also often considered an especially vulnerable group when it comes to poverty. Concerning the financial crisis it can be observed that not only private pension funds were affected by the economic downturn but also public pension schemes. Unemployment and lower earnings reduce contribution revenues of pay-as-you-go pension systems. People who are near to retirement do not have enough time for markets to recover and recoup recent investment losses in private pension funds, public pension reserves and other savings. [80] The degree to which the crisis affects current pensioners depends on the composition of their old-age income. In a number of countries, the crisis will have an impact on the level of public pensions as a result of automatic adjustment mechanisms, which could result in lower benefits. Furthermore, any voluntary retirement savings or housing assets that current pensioners were hoping to draw on during their retirement are hit by the crisis. For some pensioners, losses in these assets are substantial and interest rates are at historical lows, which may mean much low living standards in old age.[81]

When analysing the EUROSTAT data for 2007, especially in Spain the old-age poverty rate for people over 65 years (28,2%) is far higher than the poverty rate of the total population (19,7%). Surprisingly, in the immediate aftermath of the crisis the old-age poverty rate in Spain decreases by 6,5 percentage points from 28,2 per cent in 2007 to 21,7 in 2010. Sweden, on the contrary, faces the reverse trend despite having the lowest old-age poverty rate at the outbreak of the crisis. Its rate skyrockets from very low 9,9 per cent in 2007 to its highest level of 17,7 per cent in 2009 before it slightly decreases to 15,5 per cent in 2010. Austria, again, manages to have a relative balanced poverty-rate among elderly people in the immediate aftermath of the crisis. The figure changes only slightly from 14 per cent in 2007 to 15,2 per cent in 2010. In 2010, Austria's old-age poverty rate is even lower than Sweden's.

3.2.4. Poverty rate of single parents with one dependent child

Finally, the development of the poverty rates among single persons with one dependent child is highlighted. EU-wide (EU-27 and EU-15) as well as in all three countries, the poverty rates for this societal group are highest. In 2007 approximately every third single parent with a

[80] OECD (2009): 25f
[81] OECD (2009): 26f

dependent child is poor in the EU-27 and EU-15. I find it therefore necessary to analyse the development of the poverty rate among this group in the aftermath of the crisis.
In 2007, Spain's poverty rate among single persons with a dependent child is with 34,1 per cent points above the EU-27 average. Austria is only slightly lower with 31,3 per cent and Sweden has the lowest rate with 25 per cent. In Spain and Sweden the rate increases dramatically between 2007 and 2010. Sweden faces an increase of 8,1 percentage points from 25 per cent in 2007 to 33,1 per cent in 2010 while the rate in Spain increases by 11,4 percentage points from 34,1 per cent in 2007 to 45,5 per cent in 2010. Austria, on the contrary, manages to reduce its poverty rate among single parents with a dependent child by 2,9 percentage points from 31,3 per cent in 2007 to 28,2 per cent in 2010.

3.2.5. Summary of the findings concerning poverty

One might get the impression – when looking at the poverty rate of the total population - that poverty has not risen dramatically in the immediate aftermath of the outbreak of the crisis. Nevertheless, this picture is incomplete, as it does not allow differentiating between societal groups. Only when taking a closer look and asking "Who is to which extent affected by poverty?" the impact of the crisis reveals itself. The groups mostly in danger of poverty vary from country to country.
In Spain, which has significant higher poverty rates than Sweden and Austria to begin with, the level of young adults (+5,7 percentage points) and single parents with a dependent child (+ 11,4 percentage points) being at risk of poverty has risen clearly between 2007 and 2010. Although, in Sweden the lowest rates of poverty in all societal groups expect for the younger could be found in 2007, old-age poverty (+5,6 percentage points) and poverty among single parents with a dependent child (+8,1 percentage points) have risen strongly until 2010 in comparison to Austria, Spain and the EU as a whole. Austria was the one country which was able to keep its poverty rates mostly stable with the biggest increase of 1,2 percentage points among elderly people. Although, in 2010 its poverty rate among single persons with a dependent child is the lowest one out of the three countries studied and well below the EU average, it is still relatively high with 28,2 per cent illustrating that there is need for improvement.

3.3. Distribution: Developments in Sweden, Austria and Spain in comparison

So far, the economic downturn has been highlighted through the development of the unemployment rate and the risk of poverty to investigate to what extent the tax and transfer system protects individuals across different groups of society and in different European countries against income losses and unemployment. In this section changes in income distribution, measured through the Gini coefficient, which is commonly used as a measure of inequality of income or wealth, are illustrated. This part is an essential when analysing the impacts of the current crisis on European welfare states as the resulting welfare effects depend not only on the total size of losses but also on their distribution across different groups of society and the cushioning effect of the tax benefit system.[82] Furthermore, the effects of the economic crisis and austerity on inequality are of great current relevance, not only because inequality matters in its own right, but also because how the cost of the crisis is distributed has implications for the prospects for macroeconomic recovery and financial stability as well as the political acceptability of pathways in this direction.[83]

3.3.1. Which lessons can be learned from past recessions concerning distributional effects?

- Krueger et al. observe in their work the associations between inequality among working-age households and the business cycle where earnings inequality increases sharply during recessions at the bottom end of the distribution.[84] Generally speaking, inequality in disposable income during the recession rises less than inequality in earnings, reflecting the significant role played by automatic stabilizers.[85]
- Blinder and Esaki are studying the link between unemployment (and inflation) and income inequality in the USA. Their findings include one unequivocal message stating that the incidence of unemployment is quite regressive. It is estimated that each percentage point rise in the unemployment rate takes about 0.26% to 0.30% of the national income away from the lowest 40% of the income distribution and gives it to the richest 20%.[86]

[82] Cf. Dolls et al. (2011): 9
[83] Cf. Callen et al. (2011): 27
[84] Cf. Krueger et al. (2010): 8
[85] Cf. Krueger et al. (2010): 9
[86] Cf. Blinder; Esaki (1978): 607

- When Sweden was hit by severe macroeconomic shocks in the late 1980s and early 1990s unemployment rose to levels unprecedented since the depression in the 1930s.[87] As with the current recession, this crisis was initially a financial crisis, which quickly turned into a more general and major recession in Denmark, Finland, Norway and Sweden.[88] Aaberge et al. studied the consequences to the inequality of household's disposable income over this period and were struck by the absence of large increases. They observed that inequality may have responded to rising unemployment but, at most, has increased the Gini coefficient by 2 percentage points.[89]
- Latest studies from Heathcote et al confirm the link between earnings inequality and recessions at the bottom end of the distribution for the current crisis in the US. Between 2007 and 2008, earnings inequality has risen significantly with the onset of the recession.[90]

These examples clarify that, although it might be tempting to use experiences during previous recessions as a guide to the likely impact of the current recession, it is necessary to be cautious about extrapolating from the past. Muriel and Sibieta point out that 'recessions are not uniform events. Past recessions differ from each other in both their causes … and their effects' and 'trends in living standards and inequality during previous recessions reflect many other changes in public policy and other socio-economic changes, as well as what we might consider the 'direct' effects of recession'.[91] Furthermore, even among countries where there have been similarities in macroeconomic change, diversity in distributional impact can be spotted reflecting differences in socioeconomic institutions, social programmes and policy responses.[92] It is therefore necessary to turn to empirical investigations to draw conclusions about the distributional impact of the current recession.

The reader should bear in mind that the consequences of the great recession for household incomes are likely to remain for many years. Accordingly, it is important to distinguish between the immediate and longer-term impacts of the late 2000s-crisis on the distribution of income.[93] Long-term effects are not considered in this report.

[87] Cf. Aaberge et al. (2000): 79
[88] Cf. Jenkins et al. (2011): 1-22
[89] Cf. Aaberge et al. (2000): 84
[90] Cf. Heathcote et al. (2009): 43
[91] Muriel; Sibieta (2009): 15
[92] Jenkins et al. (2011): 1-2
[93] Jenkins et al. (2011): 1-2

3.3.2. Which lessons can be learned from the current crisis concerning distributional effects?

Table 12 Development of the Gini coefficient, 2007 - 2010

	Gini coefficient				%point ch
	2007	2008	2009	2010	2007-2010
EU 27	30,6	30,8	30,4	30,5	-0,1
EU 15	30,2	30,7	30,4	30,5	0,3
Spain	31,3	31,3	32,3	33,9	2,6
Austria	26,2	26,2	25,7	26,1	-0,1
Sweden	23,4	24	24,8	24,1	0,7

Source: SILC, Eurostat (online data code: ilc_di12)

The closer to zero the Gini coefficient is, the more equal the distribution. Whereas the closer to 100 per cent it is, the more unequal the distribution.[94] When investing the starting point of our analysis in the year 2007 we find that Spain suffers from the highest inequality with 31,3 per cent, Austria has a considerably lower rate of 26,2 per cent and in Sweden the Gini coefficient is the lowest with 23,4 per cent. These first insights match with the results in the literature. Jenkins et al., for example, group 21 OECD-countries accordingly to their welfare state system and identify that inequality is lowest in the Nordic countries (including Sweden), and highest in the Southern European ones (including Spain), with inequality in Western European countries in between.[95] Compared to the EU 27 or even EU 15 numbers the Gini coefficients of Sweden and Austria are far below the average whereas Spain is slightly above average (+1,1% compared to EU 15; +0,7% compared to EU 27).

When looking at the development of the Gini coefficient, in 2008 only Sweden has experienced a rise of 0,6 percentage points from 23,4 to 24 per cent while Austria and Spain have remained at their 2007-levels.

This rise in Sweden continues in 2009 from 24 per cent to 24,8 per cent. In the meantime, Spain also experiences a considerably increase of 1 percentage point from 31,3 to 32,3 per cent. Surprisingly, while one would expect the Gini coefficient to rise in the immediate aftermath of the crisis, Austria's Gini coefficient even falls half a percentage point from 26,2 per cent to 25,7 per cent. This is not only a country-specific trend, but also EU-wide a slightly decrease can be monitored. In the EU-27 the Gini coefficient decreases from 30,8 in 2008 to 30,4 per cent in 2009.

In 2010, the final year of investigation, the Gini coefficients in Sweden and Austria approach to their pre-crisis levels. From 2009 to 2010, Sweden's Gini coefficient fell 0,7 percentage

[94] Jenkins et al. (2011): 2-9
[95] Jenkins et al. (2011): 2-9f

points to 24,1 per cent. In the meantime, Austria's Gini coefficient rose to 26,1 per cent. In Spain, on the contrary, the already high gap widens even further and the upward trend continues. The Gini coefficient rises in 2010 another 1,6 percentage points leaving Spain with a Gini coefficient of 33,9 per cent in total.

3.3.3. Summary of the findings concerning the Gini coefficient

When summarising the developments concerning the Gini coefficient in the specific countries, the most conspicuous insight is the continuing upward trend in Spain widening the gap between rich and poor in fast steps. In contrast to Sweden and Austria, Spain has already had a relatively high Gini coefficient in 2007 which rose fast and steadily by 2,6 percentage points from 31,3 per cent to 33,9 per cent in 2010. Sweden experienced a rising Gini coefficient as well but after the initial sharp rise it nearly returned to its original level. Although in 2010 Sweden's Gini coefficient was 0,7 percentage points higher than before the outbreak of the crisis, it still has the most equal income distribution compared to Austria and Spain. Austria experienced a remarkable development as its Gini coefficient has not risen once between 2007 and 2010 but fell slightly with Austria's Gini coefficient in 2010 lying 0,1 percentage point beneath its pre-crisis level.

4. Summary and Conclusion

In the final conclusion the main insights concerning the developments of each country are summarised. Furthermore, the connection between specific types of welfare states and their resilience against the negative impacts of the global financial crisis are discussed.

Sweden

In an international perspective, Sweden seems to have managed to overcome the current economic crisis better than many other European states.[96] Although Swedish GDP growth rate has most drastically decreased in the immediate aftermath of the financial crisis 2008 (-5% in 2009), it has experienced the strongest rebound in 2010. Sweden was in every year - except 2009 - able to generate public balance surpluses and was, moreover, the country with the slightest decrease in its public balance. Its level of social protection spending in percentage points of GDP is the highest among our investigated countries (21,1% in 2007) but remained almost stable with only a slight increase of 0,5 percentage points between 2007 and 2010. Sweden's response to the global financial crisis was mainly to let the automatic stabilizers do their work and support employment through various activation measures.[97] Although Sweden's total unemployment and poverty rates are well below the EU15 level in all investigated years, differences in the exposure of economic shocks among societal groups can be identified.

Unemployment rose slightly to 9,1 per cent in April 2010 before decreasing. Youth unemployment increased (Youth unemployment rate: +6,1 percentage points; Youth unemployment ratio +2,9 percentage points between 2007 and 2010) and the long-term consequences of high youth unemployment remain worrying.[98] Unemployment in Sweden is highly selective according to the highest level of education attained. Graduates from university are hardly affected by unemployment (3,6% in 2007 with only a minor increase of 0,9 percentage points to 4,5% in 2010). On the contrary, unemployment levels among graduates from compulsory school are clearly above EU27 levels in all investigated years. This gap has widened in the aftermath of the crisis. Young (15-24 years) low-educated workers can be identified as one of the societal groups mostly vulnerable to the impacts of the current recession. Their unemployment rate has risen from 29,5 per cent in 2007 to 38,9 per cent in 2010.

Although unemployment levels have not experienced a drastic increase, median equivalised income has deteriorated severely between 2009 and 2010. Between 2007 and 2010, the Swedish poverty rate has faced an increase among all investigated societal groups, especially

[96] Cf. Anxo (2012): 37
[97] Cf. Kaasch et al. (2010): 17
[98] Cf. Anxo (2012): 38

among the elderly (+5,6 percentage points) and single persons with one dependent child (+8,1 percentage points). The Swedish Gini coefficient has increased by 0,7 percentage points.

Spain

Although Spain was least affected with regards to declining GDP growth rates (-3,7% in 2009), its unemployment rate has faced an early turning point (May 2007) in combination with rapid monthly expansion. Spain's government revenues therefore started deteriorating almost immediately after the outbreak of the crisis while at the same time its government expenditures have increased immensely. As more than half of those increases in spending were used for social protection (3,8 percentage points increase between 2007 and 2010) Spain's increase in expenditures in this field was highest among the three investigated countries. Because of the widening gap between decreasing revenues and increasing expenditures, Spain's public balances and its public debt have deteriorated within only a short period of time.

Youth unemployment has risen drastically between 2007 and 2010 (Youth unemployment rate: +23,4 percentage points; Youth unemployment ratio: +9,1 percentage points) and hopelessness among young people concerning the availability of jobs has more than tripled. In contrast to Sweden, rising unemployment is not restricted to low-educated workers. Unemployment among graduates from university has more than doubled between 2007 and 2010 illustrating that people from all educational levels are affected by rising unemployment.

Spain's comparatively low poverty threshold is further decreasing between 2009 and 2010. Although poverty rates for the total population have only increased by 1 percentage point between 2007 and 2010, huge variations concerning different societal groups can be identified. Whereas the poverty rate among elderly decreased by 6,5 percentage points, it increased by 5,7 percentage points among young people and by 11,4 percentage points among single parents with one dependent child. Spain's experienced the highest increase in its Gini coefficient among our investigated countries (2,6 percentage points within only four years).

Austria

Despite the massive blow, the Austrian economy still performed better than many other European economies.[99] The deterioration of Austria's public balances has been less pronounced compared to EU27 developments. Whereas Sweden and Spain were confronted with shrinking revenues, Austria's worsening public balances were mainly due to higher levels of expenditure (+4 percentage points between 2007 and 2010) in the immediate aftermath of the crisis. Austria's unemployment level for the total population as well as for the younger workforce experienced only minor increases. Whereas Spain and Sweden had to fight against rapidly rising unemployment levels among young graduates from compulsory school, Austria even managed to decrease unemployment in this societal group.

Although the poverty rate of the total population remains almost stable, subtle gradations among societal groups can be identified. Poverty rates among young and elderly people have risen slightly, whereas a decrease could be monitored among single parents with one dependent child. Austria was the only country among the three countries that even experienced a slight decrease in its Gini coefficient between 2007 and 2010.

Connection between welfare regimes and resilience

Sweden, representing the social democratic welfare state, and Austria, representing the corporatist welfare state, had already well-established welfare regimes before the outbreak of the financial crisis. The social protection in the familialist welfare state of Spain, in contrast, is fragmented and welfare state institutions seem highly inefficient.

Both, Sweden and Austria, had relatively high levels of social protection expenditure when the crisis hit. Consequently they had to increase it considerably less than Spain in the aftermath of the financial crisis. It is noteworthy, however, that Austria and Spain, have been hit harder in terms of maximum decline in GDP growth rate but their economies have experienced comparatively strong rebounds.

Although the number of investigated countries is too limited to make profound statements about the connection between a specific type of welfare regime and impacts of recessions, the results of this book underline previous findings.

To begin with, it could be observed when monitoring the development of the unemployment rate and the poverty rate, that countries and their inhabitants are differently exposed to economic shocks due to the variations in the design of social security that they are covered with. Typically, recessions reduce incomes and raise poverty rates.[100] The stabilisation of the household income distribution is an achievable goal in the face of macroeconomic turbulenc-

[99] Cf. Hermann; Flecker (2012): 123

[100] Jenkins et al. (2011): 9-1

es, at least in the short term. However, the degree of distributional stabilisation is associated with already having a relatively strong welfare state in general and social safety nets in particular.[101] Furthermore, it has to be considered that the government's ability for intervention is primarily restricted to the instruments available.[102] On the basis of this general idea the question rises, whether resilience against the crisis can be linked with the welfare state typology and if one type of welfare state has been more effective in cushioning the negative impacts from the financial crisis for its inhabitants.

This analysis does not intend to compare the welfare states and the intensity with which they have been hit by the crisis on scales of more or less as this would oversimplify a very complex issue. However, it can be monitored that less developed welfare states have to react in more active ways to crises, as was the case with Spain in the current recession.[103] This is due to particular gaps in social protection as well as less established automatic fiscal stabilisation.[104] This can be illustrated by the developments in Spain. First, until May 2010, the crisis in Spain was considered as a temporary economic downturn that could simply be overcome using measured dealing with current circumstances.[105] But the short- and medium-term prospects are grim. Banyuls and Recio point out that the labour reforms will lead to increased inequality and further falling wages. The public spending cuts are increasing unemployment and precariousness in new industries especially for employees with higher education, while slowing down economic activity and creating worse living conditions and support for families.[106]

This illustrates that it is a necessary imperative to have schemes implemented already before an economic downturn shows its first consequences for the individual and society as a whole.[107] Finally, in the aftermath of the crisis it is essential to realize that, contrary to earlier beliefs, social protection does not constitute an economic handicap nor does it bear any responsibility for the causes of the crisis.[108] Above all, the economic crisis has come at the right time to recall and to demonstrate that high levels of social protection cushion economic recession and reduce its impacts.[109]

101 Jenkins et al. (2011): 9-8
102 Cf. ILO (2010a): 107
103 Cf. Kaasch et al. (2010): 18
104 Cf. Kaasch et al. (2010): 18
105 Cf. Banyuls; Recio (2012): 208
106 Cf. Banyuls; Recio (2012): 214
107 Cf. ILO (2010a): 105
108 Cf. Euzéby (2010): 71
109 Euzéby (2010): 81

Bibliography

Aaberge, Rolf; Björklund, Anders; Jäntti, Markus; Pedersen, Peder J.; Smith, Nina; Wennemo, Tom (2000): Unemployment shocks and income distribution: how did the Nordic countries fare during their crises?, in: The Scandinavian Journal of Economics, 2000/Vol. 102, No. 1, pp. 77 – 99
Online available: http://www.jstor.org/stable/3440706 (accessed 28.10.2012)

Anxo, Dominique (2012): From one crisis to another: the Swedish model in turbulent times revisited, in Lehndorff, Steffen (ed.): A triumph of failed ideas. European models of capitalism in the crisis. Brussels: ETUI, p. 27 - 40

Arts, Wil; Gelissen, John (2002): Three worlds of welfare capitalism or more? A state-of-the-art report, in: Journal of European Social Policy; 2002/Vol. 12, No. 2, pp. 137 – 158
Online available: http://esp.sagepub.com/content/12/2/137.abstract

Aven, Terje (2011): On Some Recent Definitions and Analysis Frameworks for Risk, Vulnerability, and Resilience, in: Risk Analysis: An International Journal; 2001/Vol. 4, No. 8, pp. 515-522

Baldwin, Peter (1996): Can We Define a European Welfare State Model?, in Greve, Bent (ed.) Comparative Welfare Systems: the Scandinavian Model in a Period of Change, London: Macmillan. pp. 29–44

Banyuls, Joseph; Recio, Albert (2012): Spain: the nightmare of Mediterranean neoliberalism, in Lehndorff, Steffen (ed.): A triumph of failed ideas. European models of capitalism in the crisis. Brussels: ETUI, p. 199 – 218

Behrendt, Christina; Bonnet, Florence; Cichon, Michael; Hagemejer, Krzysztof (2011): Social Security: Three lessons from the global crisis, in: The global Crisis. Causes, responses and challenges, Geneva: International Labour Office, pp. 167 - 180
Online available:
http://www.ilo.org/wcmsp5/groups/public/@dgreports/@dcomm/@publ/documents/publication/wcms_155824.pdf

Blinder, Alan S.; Esaki, Howard Y. (1978): Macroeconomic activity and income distribution in the postwar United States, in The Review of Economics and Statistics, 1978/Vol. 60, No. 4, pp. 604 – 609
Online available: http://www.jstor.org/stable/10.2307/1924254 (accessed 28.10.2012)

Bonoli, Giuliano (1997): Classifying Welfare States: a Two-dimension Approach, in: Journal of Social Policy, 1997/Vol. 26, No. 3: pp. 351 – 372

Burns, Arthur F.; Wesley, C. Mitchell (1946): Measuring Business Cycles. New York, New York: National Bureau of Economic Research

Callan, Tim, Chrysa Leventi, Horacio Levy, Manos Matsaganis, Alari Paulus, and Holly Sutherland (2011): The distributional effects of austerity measures: a comparison of six EU countries. Dublin, European Commission

Carpenter, Steve; Walker, Brian J.; Anderies, Marty; Abel, Nick (2001): From Metaphor to Measurement: Resilience of What to What? In ECOSYSTEMS, 2001/Vol. 4, No. 8, pp.

765-781 Online available: http://link.springer.com/article/10.1007%2Fs10021-001-0045-9

Claessens, Stijn; Dell'Ariccia, Giovanni; Igan, Deniz; Laeven Luc (2010): Cross-country experiences and policy implications from the global financial crisis, in: Economic Policy, 2010/Vol. 25, No. 62, pp. 267 – 293

Die Zeit: Mayrbäurl, Cornelia (13.01.2012): Schleichende Apokalypse. http://www.zeit.de/2012/03/A-Analyse, (accessed 28.10.2012)

Dolls, Mathias.; Fuest, Clemens.; Peichl, Andreas (2011): Automatic Stabilizers, Economic Crisis and Income Distribution in Europe. Amsterdam, AIAS, Gini Discussion Paper 23 Online available: http://www.gini-research.org/system/uploads/295/original/DP_23_-_Dolls_Fuest_Peichl.pdf?1331234943 (accessed 28.10.2012)

Esping-Andersen, Gøsta (1990): Three worlds of welfare capitalism. Cambridge: Polity Press Online available: http://de.scribd.com/doc/77492704/Esping-Andersen-The-Three-Worlds-of-Welfare-Capitalism-1990

Esping-Andersen, Gøsta (1997): Hyprid or Unique? The Japanese Welfare State between Europe and America', in: Journal of European Social Policy, 1997/Vol. 7, No. 3, pp. 179-189

Eurostat a): General government expenditure statistics. http://epp.eurostat.ec.europa.eu/statistics_explained/index.php/General_government_expenditure_statistics (accessed 28.10.2012)

Eurostat b): Unemployment - LFS ajustes series. http://epp.eurostat.ec.europa.eu/cache/ITY_SDDS/en/une_esms.htm (accessed 28.10.2012)

Eurostat c) Definitions http://epp.eurostat.ec.europa.eu/portal/page/portal/employment_unemployment_lfs/methodology/definitions; (28.11.2012)

Eurostat d): Unemployment Statistics http://epp.eurostat.ec.europa.eu/statistics_explained/index.php/Unemployment_statistics#Further_Eurostat_information (accessed 28.10.2012)

Eurostat (2009): Hijman, Remko: Statistics in focus, Population and social conditions, 53/2009 http://epp.eurostat.ec.europa.eu/cache/ITY_OFFPUB/KS-SF-09-053/EN/KS-SF-09-053-EN.PDF (accessed 28.10.2012)

Eurostat (2010): Eurostat newsrelease. Living conditions in 2008. online available: http://epp.eurostat.ec.europa.eu/cache/ITY_PUBLIC/3-18012010-AP/EN/3-18012010-AP-EN.PDF (accessed 28.10.2012)

Euzéby, Alain (2010): Economic crisis and social protection in the European Union: Moving beyond immediate responses, in: International Social Security Review, 2010/Vol. 63, No. 2, pp. 71 – 86

Ferrera, Maurizio (1996): The “Southern” Model of Welfare in Social Europe, in: Journal of European Social Policy, 1996/Vol. 6, No. 1, pp. 17 – 37

Figari, Francesco; Salvatori, Sutherland, Holly; Tumino, Alberto (2010): The economic downturn, unemployment and risk of poverty: stress testing European welfare systems. Dublin: European commission

Financial Times: Hill, Steven (24.06.2012): Youth unemployment is bad but not as bad as we’re told. Online available: http://www.ft.com/intl/cms/s/0/5cc9db3e-bbbc-11e1-9436-00144feabdc0.html#axzz2BC44nVFo (accessed 28.10.2012)

Gabler Verlag (Herausgeber), Gabler Wirtschaftslexikon, Stichwort: Depression; online available:
http://wirtschaftslexikon.gabler.de/Archiv/54616/depression-v4.html (accessed 28.11.2012)

Gourevitch, Peter (1986): Politics in Hard Times: Comparative Responses to International Economic Crisis. Ithaca: Cornell University Press

Heathcote, Jonathan; Perri, Fabrizio; Giovanni, L.Violante (2009): Unequal We Stand: An Empirical Analysis of Economic Inequality in the United States, 1967-2006. NBER Working Paper No. 15483, November 2009. online available: http://www.nber.org/papers/w15483.pdf?new_window=1 (accessed 28.10.2012)

Hermann, Christoph; Flecker, Jörg (2012): The Austrian model and the financial and economic crisis, in Lehndorff, Steffen (ed.): A triumph of failed ideas. European models of capitalism in the crisis. Brussels: ETUI, p. 121 – 136

Holling, Crawford Stanley (1973): Resilience and Stability of Ecological Systems, in: Annual Review of Ecology and Systematics, 1973/Vol. 4, pp. 1-23; online available: http://webarchive.iiasa.ac.at/Admin/PUB/Documents/RP-73-003.pdf (accessed 28.10.2012)

ILO (2012): The youth unemployment crisis: Time for action. Report V. International Labour Conference, 101st Session 2012; Geneva: International Labour Office; online available: http://www.ilo.org/public/libdoc/ilo/2012/112B09_39_engl.pdf (accessed 28.10.2012)

Jenkins, Stephan P.; Brandolini, Andrea; Micklewright, John; Nolan, Brian (2011): The Great Recession and the Distribution of Household Income. Presented at ‘Incomes Across the Great Recession’, XIII European Conference of the Fondazione Rodolfo Debenedetti, Palermo, 10 September 2011

Jones, Barry (ed.)(2001): Routledge Encyclopedia of International Political Economy. Vol. 1, A-F, London: Routledge

Kaasch, Alexandra; Starke, Peter; Van Hooren, Franca (2010): The Welfare State as Crisis Manager? Comparing Social Policy Responses to Three Major Economic Crisis. Bremen: Universität Bremen

Kaminsky, Graciela L.; Reinhart, Carmen M.; Végh, Carlos A. (2003): The Unholy Trinity of Financial Contagion, in: Journal of Economic Perspectives, 2003/Vol. 17, No. 4, pp. 51 – 74

Online available: http://homepages.wmich.edu/~balik/VSE/JEPContagion.pdf (accessed 28.10.2012)

Karamessini, Maria (2007): The Southern European social model: Changes and continuities in recent decades, Geneva: International Institute for Labour Studies; online available: http://www.ilo.org/public/english/bureau/inst/publications/discussion/dp17407.pdf (accessed 28.10.2012)

Konkolewsky, Hans-Horst (2009): Social security systems: Responding to the crisis, In: Social Policy Highlight 10, International Social Security Association, Geneva; online available: http://news.issa.int/eng/newsletter/newsletter_repository/alerts/en/new_publication_social_policy_highlight_responding_to_the_crisis (accessed 28.10.2012)

Krueger, Dirk; Perri, Fabrizio; Fistaferri, Luigi; Violante, Giovanni L. (2010): Cross-sectional facts for macroeconomists, in: Review of Economic Dynamics, 2010/Vol. 13, No. 1, pp. 1 – 14
Online available: http://www.sciencedirect.com/science/article/pii/S1094202509000726 (accessed 28.10.2012)

Lehndorff, Steffen (ed.)(2012): A triumph of failed ideas. European models of capitalism in the crisis. Brussels: ETUI

Lehndorff, Steffen (2012): Introduction – the triumph of failed ideas; in Lehndorff, Steffen (ed.): A triumph of failed ideas. European models of capitalism in the crisis. Brussels: ETUI, p. 7 -26

Leibfried, Stephan (1992): Towards a European welfare state? On Integrating Poverty Regimes into the European Community, in: Ferge, Zsuzsa; Kolberg, Jon Eiving (eds): Social Policy in a Changing Europe. Frankfurt am Main: Campus Verlag

Letschke, Janine; Theodoropoulou, Sotiria; Watt, Andrew (2012): How do economic governance reforms and austerity measures affect inclusive growth as formulated in the Europe 2020 Strategy?, in Lehndorff, Steffen (ed.): A triumph of failed ideas. European models of capitalism in the crisis. Brussels: ETUI, p. 7-26

Muriel, Alastair; Sibieta, Luke (2009): Living Standards During Previous Recessions, Briefing Note BN85. London: Institute for Fiscal Studies. Online available: http://www.ifs.org.uk/bns/bn85.pdf (accessed 28.10.2012)

NBER (National Bureau of Economic Research): US Business Cycle Expansion and Contractions: http://www.nber.org/cycles.html (accessed 28.10.2012)

OECD (2009): Pensions at a Glance 2009. Retirement-Income systems in OECD countries; online available: http://www.oecd-ilibrary.org/docserver/download/8109081e.pdf?expires=1354198037&id=id&accname=guest&checksum=F82D7F36A24049E9B0139D4B0CE98874 (accessed 28.11.2012)

Özdemir, Erhan; Sanoussi, Fadila; Ward, Terry (2010): The potential effects of recession on the risk of poverty. Dublin: European Commission

Reinhart, Carmen M; Rogoff, Kenneth S. (2009): This time is different: eight centuries of finanical folly; Princeton University Press, Princeton

Starke, Peter; Kaasch, Alexandra; Van Horren, Franca (2011): Explaining the variety of social policy responses to economic crisis: How parties and welfare state structure interact. Sonderforschungsbericht 597 „Staatlichkeit im Wandel", Bremen: Universität Bremen Online available: http://econstor.eu/bitstream/10419/50561/1/670086355.pdf

Trifiletti, Rossana (1999): Southern European Welfare Regimes and the Worsening Position of Women, in: Journal of European Social Policy, 1999/Vol. 9, No. 1, pp 49 – 64 Online available: http://esp.sagepub.com/content/9/1/49.short

von Kempski, Jürgen (1972) 'Zur Logik der Ordungsbegriffe, besonders in den Sozialwissenschaften', in H. Albert (ed.) Theorie und Realität. Ausgewählte Aufsätze zur Wissenschaftslehre der Sozialwissenschaften, pp. 115–38. Tübingen: J. C. B. Mohr (Paul Siebeck).

Appendix

Appendix 1: Unemployment rate: monthly average, seasonally adjusted date, total population up to 74 years; 2007 – 2010

	Jan. 07	**Feb.07**	**Mar. 07**	**Apr. 07**	**May 07**	**June 07**	**July 07**	**Aug. 07**	**Sep. 07**	**Oct. 07**	**Nov. 07**	**Dec. 07**
EU 27	7,6	7,5	7,4	7,3	7,3	7,2	7,2	7,2	7,1	7	7	6,9
EU 15	7,4	7,3	7,3	7,2	7,1	7,1	7,1	7,1	7	7	6,9	6,9
SP	8,2	8,1	8	7,9	7,9	8,1	8,3	8,5	8,5	8,5	8,6	8,8
AT	4,4	4,3	4,4	4,6	4,6	4,5	4,7	4,7	4,4	4,2	4,1	4,1
SE	6,6	6,2	6,5	6,1	5,9	6,2	5,8	6	6,1	6,2	6	6
	Jan. 08	**Feb. 08**	**Mar. 08**	**Apr. 08**	**May 08**	**June 08**	**July 08**	**Aug. 08**	**Sep. 08**	**Oct. 08**	**Nov. 08**	**Dec. 08**
EU 27	6,9	6,8	6,8	6,8	6,9	7	7	7,1	7,2	7,3	7,5	7,7
EU 15	6,9	6,9	6,8	6,9	7	7,2	7,2	7,3	7,3	7,5	7,7	8
SP	9	9,2	9,3	9,9	10,5	11	11,4	11,8	12,3	13,2	14	14,9
AT	4,1	4	3,7	3,5	3,5	3,5	3,6	3,8	3,7	3,7	4,1	4,4
SE	6	5,8	5,8	5,8	5,8	6,6	6,2	5,9	6,4	6,3	7	6,8
	Jan. 09	**Feb. 09**	**Mar. 09**	**Apr. 09**	**May 09**	**June 09**	**July 09**	**Aug. 09**	**Sep. 09**	**Oct. 09**	**Nov. 09**	**Dec. 09**
EU 27	8,1	8,4	8,6	8,8	8,9	9,1	9,2	9,3	9,4	9,4	9,5	9,5
EU 15	8,3	8,6	8,8	9	9,1	9,3	9,3	9,4	9,5	9,5	9,5	9,5
SP	15,9	16,8	17,4	17,7	17,9	18	18,3	18,5	18,8	18,9	19	19,2
AT	4,3	4,3	4,6	4,8	4,7	5	5	5	5,2	5,1	4,8	4,6
SE	6,8	7,7	7,8	7,8	8,9	8,4	8,4	8,8	8,7	8,7	8,7	8,9
	Jan. 10	**Feb.10**	**March 10**	**Apr. 10**	**May 10**	**June 10**	**July 10**	**Aug. 10**	**Sep. 10**	**Oct. 10**	**Nov. 10**	**Dec. 10**
EU 27	9,6	9,7	9,7	9,7	9,7	9,6	9,6	9,6	9,6	9,6	9,6	9,6
EU 15	9,6	9,6	9,6	9,7	9,7	9,6	9,6	9,6	9,6	9,6	9,5	9,5
SP	19,2	19,4	19,6	19,9	20,1	20,2	20,2	20,3	20,4	20,5	20,5	20,5
AT	4,4	4,5	4,6	4,6	4,5	4,4	4,5	4,5	4,3	4,1	4,1	4,2
SE	8,9	8,8	8,5	9,1	8,5	8,1	8,5	8,2	8,2	8	7,8	7,8

*Source: Eurostat (*une_rt_m)

SP … Spain

AT .. Austria

SE … Sweden

Appendix 2: Unemployment rate: monthly average, seasonally adjusted date, population under the age of 25 years, 2007 – 2010

	Jan. 07	**Feb. 07**	**Mar. 07**	**Apr. 07**	**May 07**	**June 07**	**July 07**	**Aug. 07**	**Sep. 07**	**Oct. 07**	**Nov. 07**	**Dec. 07**
EU 27	16,5	16,2	16	15,8	15,7	15,8	15,7	15,7	15,4	15,3	15,1	15,1
EU 15	16,1	15,7	15,5	15,5	15,3	15,4	15,3	15,4	15,1	15,3	15,1	15,2
SP	17,6	17,4	17,4	17,6	17,5	18,2	18,4	18,7	18,7	18,6	19,1	19,7
AT	7,9	8	8,7	9,6	9,3	9,1	9,9	9,6	8,5	8,4	7,9	7,4
SE	19	20,1	20,2	17,2	18,6	19,8	17,5	18,8	19,5	20,7	18,5	19,3
	Jan. 08	**Feb. 08**	**Mar. 08**	**Apr. 08**	**May 08**	**June 08**	**July 08**	**Aug. 08**	**Sep. 08**	**Oct. 08**	**Nov. 08**	**Dec. 08**
EU 27	15,1	15	15,1	15,2	15,4	15,7	15,8	15,9	16,2	16,5	17,1	17,4
EU 15	15,1	15,1	15	15,2	15,5	15,8	15,9	16,1	16,4	16,8	17,4	17,8
SP	20,4	20,7	21	22,3	23,2	24,1	24,6	25,1	26	28,1	29,8	31,4
AT	8,3	8,3	7,4	6,8	7,1	7,2	7	7,4	8	8,6	9,8	10,3
SE	19,4	18,1	19,2	19	18	23,9	21,2	18,2	20,7	19,5	23,1	20,3
	Jan. 09	**Feb. 09**	**Mar. 09**	**Apr. 09**	**May 09**	**June 09**	**July 09**	**Aug. 09**	**Sep. 09**	**Oct. 09**	**Nov. 09**	**Dec. 09**
EU 27	18,1	18,8	19,3	19,7	19,9	20,2	20,6	20,8	21	21,1	21	21,1
EU 15	18,5	19	19,5	19,8	19,9	20,2	20,5	20,5	20,8	21	20,8	20,8
SP	33,3	34,9	36,1	36,6	37,2	37,8	39,1	39,7	40,1	39,9	39,5	39,7
AT	9,4	8,8	9,5	10	10,1	10,8	10,7	10,2	10,1	10,4	9,8	9,6
SE	22,1	23,5	21,8	23,3	27,4	24	27	28,1	25,2	26,4	25,2	25,9
	Jan. 10	**Feb. 10**	**March 10**	**Apr. 10**	**May 10**	**June 10**	**July 10**	**Aug. 10**	**Sep. 10**	**Oct. 10**	**Nov. 10**	**Dec. 10**
EU 27	21,1	21,4	21,1	21,2	22,1	20,9	20,9	20,8	21	21	21	21,1
EU 15	20,8	20,9	20,6	20,9	20,8	20,6	20,6	20,6	20,6	20,5	20,4	20,4
SP	39,7	40,1	40,3	40,8	41,2	41,5	41,7	41,9	42,2	42,9	43,4	43,7
AT	9,5	9,5	9	8,5	9	8,7	8,7	9,6	9,1	7,7	8,1	8,2
SE	27,4	25,6	25,9	27,5	24,9	24,6	25,5	24,6	24,8	23,9	22,5	24,2

*Source: Eurostat (*une_rt_m)